ONE
WOMAN'S
JOURNEY
FROM
CANCER TO
HOPE

Jeana Floyd
with Erin Keely Marshall

An Uninvited Guest

FOREWORD BY JOHNELLE HUNT
co-founder of J.B. Hunt Trucking

_____

presented to

_____

from

_____

date

Written with Erin Keeley Marshall, www.erinkeeleymarshall.net
Cover and interior design by Rebekah Krall

ISBN-13: 978-0-89221-663-5
ISBN-10: 0-89221-664-6
Library of Congress Number: 2007925419

Printed in Italy

New Leaf Press
A Division of New Leaf Publishing Group

Dedication

Without the encouragement from my husband, Ronnie, this book would never have been written. So much a part of his character, Ronnie made sure that I received the very best treatment and care. He was by my side throughout the entire journey, and he is the one who has gently encouraged me to "tell my story." It's finally happened — and now I dedicate this book to him. I am so grateful to the Lord for the additional years He has given Ronnie and me. Not only did the Lord answer my prayers to get to see Josh and Nick grow up, but also to see them marry their precious wives, Kate and Meredith, and now even the blessing of my sweet grandchildren!

Table of Contents

Foreword

I have been blessed to have some very unique and wonderful ladies in my life, many of whom I call my friends. Jeana Floyd is one of these. I remember when we first met; she was the wife of our dynamic young pastor. Her sweet, quiet spirit was a wonderful complement to her husband and she served him and all of us in the congregation well as she mothered her two young sons and met all the demands of a growing church so graciously that she made it look effortless. Obviously, it was not. We immediately took her into our hearts and loved her for her genuineness and servant's heart. Imagine our devastation when we heard she had breast cancer. I am sure we were not as stunned as her family, but nearly so.

Our hearts ached with unbelief as we began to pray for her recovery. I thought I knew Jeana Floyd, but as I watched her on this journey of faith and recovery, I realized that I had no idea the strength and courage that dwelt in that diminutive little frame. Her courage was only surpassed by her faith. It was an awesome scene to watch.

As she traveled the hills and valleys of cancer treatment, she kept her sweet spirit. I am sure that there were discouraging and pain-filled days, but her smile never wavered. She was confident in her God, and was probably unaware of the great example of grace she was setting for all around her.

Years have past since Jeana's victorious battle with cancer. She is a most beautiful grandmother with that same sweet unwavering smile. She has been through the valley and has emerged with that enviable graciousness and patience produced by the endurance of great trials.

There is a term used these days to describe incredible, unflappable valor… "grace under fire." Well I have seen "grace under fire" and her name is Jeana. I am so proud to call her my friend.

Johnelle Hunt
Co-founder of the J. B. Hunt Trucking

A Note to My Readers

I'll never get over having cancer. Even though it's been almost 18 years now, I'll never "get over" that time in my life. I've asked God to never let me forget what it was like. You don't go through something like cancer and just forget it happened. It forever changed me — and it was not all bad. I learned some very valuable lessons through it.

Most days that season seems like a lifetime ago, but occasionally it feels like yesterday. My first thought each morning is no longer, *I have cancer*. Most times I wake up feeling overwhelmed by the activities ahead of me. But sometimes I still remember those emotions of having cancer, and I am flooded with gratitude that I am still here. At the most inconspicuous moments, I experience overwhelming joy of simply being alive, able to "be and do" the daily details of life. This usually comes to me when I am alone — pushing my cart in a parking lot, heading to my car, feeling the wind blow through my hair. Such insignificant daily tasks, but done with such gratitude for life and breath.

God answered my prayer and allowed me to see my sons, Josh and Nick, grow up, and my husband, Ronnie, and I will celebrate 31 years of marriage in December 2007. Not only that, I have two precious daughters-in-law, Kate and Meredith, and three sweet grandchildren. I am a blessed woman in so many ways.

Part of the blessing was having cancer, even though it was one of the most painful times I've experienced. It gave me an understanding of pain and brokenness that I had never experienced. And yes, there are many things worse than cancer, but it was the venue God used to mold me and stretch me in new ways.

I asked God to never let me forget how badly you can hurt — the brokenness, the fear of the unknown — so that I might be used to encourage others in their own pain, whatever the "label of pain" may be. So even though I am way past diagnosis, treatment, and recovery, having cancer is still very much with me and will forever be a part of who I am.

I pray you will be blessed in some way by my story. I thought I knew God's faithfulness before my cancer, but now I understand what it's like to hang on to His promises as if life depends on them.

Because it does.

May you experience the comfort of being in His hand as you journey through your own life.

– Jeana

It is good for me that I have been afflicted, that I may learn Your statutes.
Psalm 119:71; NKJV

part one

MY STORY

Praise be to the God and Father of
our Lord Jesus Christ, the Father of
compassion and the God of all comfort,
who comforts us in all our troubles,
so that we can comfort those in any
trouble with the comfort we ourselves
have received from God.

2 CORINTHIANS 1:3–4; NIV

Jeana Floyd

ONE *I Prayed for This?*

Trust in him at all times, O people; pour out your hearts to him, for God is our refuge.
PSALM 62:8; NIV

God's Unique Answer

Some people say to be careful what you pray for because you just might get it. Those same people might view my journey through breast cancer as God's mixed-up answer to my prayers for a less cluttered life. After all, no one asks for sickness. And who would imagine that He'd use something like cancer to show me new levels of His peace and hope . . . and even joy?

Surely not me.

But that's just what He did. If that sounds too good to be true, rest assured I say it with complete honesty. God makes no mistakes, and He allows no sorrow without a purpose. I grew in unexpected ways through having cancer. While it was a journey I am glad to have behind me, it is one I do feel grateful for.

It began in the late 1980s. Raising two young boys and sharing in ministry as a pastor's wife, I enjoyed having my hands full and my schedule busy. However, as we approached the 1989 holiday season, I found myself craving simplicity. As is common in the western world, it's easy for my husband, Ronnie, and me to get caught in the trappings of our calling. We love to give of our time, and we cherish our church, but we often find ourselves long on commitments and short on rest and relaxation. Anyone in full-time ministry can tell you it makes for a somewhat complicated lifestyle.

While the dust settled after busy Christmas and New Year's celebrations, I found myself reflecting on the previous year's harried schedule that had slowly taken its toll on me. As the first days of January ushered in a new year, I craved simplicity for the coming months, so I asked God to remove the excess clutter from my life. Where was I overbooked, overwhelmed, overstressed? I had several ideas for how He could answer my request.

Not one of them included a cancerous lump in my breast.

An Uninvited Guest

I had actually found the lump a couple of years earlier when we lived in Texas. A preliminary visit to the doctor gave me small comfort when I was told it likely was

nothing of concern — just fibrocystic breast disease. My doctor recommended a mammogram and simply told me to watch it.

However, in the closing weeks of 1989, I knew the lump had changed, and my apprehension grew with it. You may identify with the initial twinge of fear I felt. Something wasn't quite right about that lump. When the nagging feeling persisted, I sought out a doctor friend, Dr. John Kendrick, at church, who had offered to perform a biopsy after the new year. So we crossed into 1990, and I sat in his office on January 15.

Ronnie and I heard the news that very day. In my mind that morning, this was going to be an insignificant interruption in my busy schedule, and I also didn't want to throw a kink into Ronnie's busy schedule — but thankfully, he sensed the need to be there. He sat in the waiting room during the procedure as the morning sun crept higher over the horizon. When the doctor requested to see him privately, he knew something was going on.

"Jeana has cancer."

When people talk about hearing "those three little words," most times they're referring to a warm, fuzzy "I love you." Both messages are life-changing, but oh, they're worlds apart in meaning.

Although I was the patient, Ronnie took the initial blow and felt the first weight of enormous fear. He and the doctor waited while the anesthetic wore off, and then told me the news together. The lump was malignant.

Even now, it doesn't make sense to my human mind. There was no earthly reason why I should have that disease. At 35 years old, I was the picture of health. I had done everything right. I had no family history of breast cancer at that time. I took care of myself, I'd nursed my sons, and Ronnie and I walked three miles a day. Plus, I had many responsibilities and no time for a sickness hiatus.

But cancer does not distinguish between the too young, too healthy, or too busy. Sure enough, it had knocked on my door. And naturally, it was a very unwelcome visitor.

On our way home from the doctor's office, Ronnie and I agreed on a plan for sharing the news. Being the leaders of a large congregation, we wanted to nip rumors in the bud by telling our church as soon as possible. We wanted them to hear the whole truth from us, and we knew we would need their prayers and practical support through whatever struggles the next few months, or years, would bring. We also decided to tell our sons Josh and Nick, who were a mere nine and six at the time. Their stable world inevitably would be rocked to some extent while their parents reeled from shock and learned to live in survival mode through a season of treatment we had yet to decide upon.

Originally from Texas, Ronnie and I knew we wanted to seek treatment advice from M.D. Anderson Hospital in Houston. We'd visited many patients there in previous years and knew of its world-renowned reputation. So we made the first of two trips soon after the biopsy and ended up following their advice for a rigorous treatment, which included a lumpectomy, followed by six weeks of radiation, followed by six months of chemotherapy.

There it was. *Chemotherapy* . . . a word I dreaded hearing, let alone experiencing. It was my greatest fear — the poison, the sickness, the nausea. All of it for the intentional purpose of killing off the sick parts of me to save the rest of me.

My other greatest fear was losing my hair, something I knew chemo often caused. Like many people, my hair is my subconscious "crown," as the Bible calls it (Prov. 16:31; Song of Sol. 7:5). It is a protection and a covering. I didn't view my fears of losing my hair as shallow or prideful. I was simply a normal, red-blooded woman who found a measure of self-worth in my appearance. God created women to reflect His beauty. Could I do that bald? Was my hair really a part of the "clutter" that needed to go?

I did not understand the whys of it all, but I had enough background with God to know that He was about to lead me on a path of deeper faith as I lived each day watching Him unfold a suddenly uncertain future.

February 15, 1990 . . . A month ago today we found out I had breast cancer. This past month has been a mirage of events — 2 trips to M.D. Anderson, surgery, and now I have begun radiation treatment. I can't

remember everything — it has all happened so fast — many emo-
tions to deal with. God has been gracious through it all. It's still really
hard to believe this is happening to me. I look around at NARTI (North-
west Arkansas Radiation Therapy Institute) and everyone is at least 70 or
80 years old & I wonder, "What am I doing here? I don't belong here!!"
Today I feel very strong & positive. Every day has not been so easy. Some
days I have felt as though my heart would break in two. . . . Today, on
a day when I feel happy & think I can handle anything (even losing my
hair!), I want the Lord to know my heart. Other days I may not be strong.
Lord, I want to experience all you have for me during this time. I want
to walk with you in a new way. Change my perspective — you already
have in so many ways. Keep me pure & loving, not filled with bitterness.
Keep my heart tender. Thank you for reassurance in your Word & for
the wonderful people you have sent to minister to me. May my life truly
be a testimony of your grace. I pray I will learn the lessons you have for
me — gracefully. I want to walk through this gracefully. Let beauty from
inside glow. May I radiate with your love so clearly that even in illness you
can shine through. . . . Give me courage to walk through days of suffering.
Give me courage & self-control when my hair falls out. Do a work within
me so that I may be able to accept your perfect will. Give Ronnie the same
courage & grace to walk through this with me.

Lord, I even think today I can thank you for this. What an opportunity to know you better — praise the Lord! You have chosen me for this special time.

Father, protect my children from <u>fear</u> — fear of many things. May all of us grow more deeply in love with one another. In some ways I feel like I'm going on a year-long retreat. Where will I be this time next year?

As our world became swallowed up in cancer talk and cancer thought, no one in our family escaped scot-free from cancer fears.

Ronnie claimed a Scripture for me and carried it on a note card in his pocket throughout my treatment. It speaks of God's presence no matter what catastrophes we face:

Do not fear, for I have redeemed you; I have called you by name; you are Mine! When you pass through the waters, I will be with you; And through the rivers, they will not overflow you. When you walk through the fire, you will not be scorched, nor will the flame burn you. For I am the LORD your God, the Holy One of Israel, your Savior. Isaiah 43:1–3; NASB

As for our kids, we tried to share just enough details to let them know what was happening, or going to happen, just before the actual event so they didn't have time to get caught up in fears of the unknown. Still, we had no real control over what went through their young minds.

I recently asked them what they remember about those days.

Josh told me, "I remember being very scared at first. I know that I asked Dad if you were going to die from this. He said no, and that the medicine was going to help you."

And Nick remembers the night we told them. He added, "I can remember Josh [later] asking, 'Why can't they give her all the medicine at the same time?' to which Dad responded, 'Because it would kill her.' That's the first time I think I realized it was serious."

They remember the wig and turbans, trips to NARTI, even eating Happy Meals with the nurses.

Somehow life continued as the days crept through my treatment, despite our fears and lack of control over much of its daily pace and its outcome. That's God's sovereign faithfulness. *He* remained in control as He sent daily lessons about what it means to let go and rest in His wisdom and care.

In His quiet, relentless way, God led me through my fears.

TWO   *Letting Go and Leaning*

Let him who walks in the dark, who has no light, trust in the name of the LORD and rely on his God.

ISAIAH 50:10; NIV

Journaling

> February 22, 1990
>
> *Peace comes from within. You can be comforted, encouraged, loved, and even sheltered (somewhat) by others (and God, too). But true peace comes only from the Lord. I have had an incredible amount of peace the past two weeks. I feel full of joy — anxious to live each day to the fullest. Only <u>rarely</u> have I slipped into fear (or wondering "Why is this happening?") during recent days. . . . But I left the surgical clinic today wondering, "Why did <u>I</u> get the news I got?"*

But as the 19th-century preacher Charles Haddon Spurgeon said, "God is
too good to be unkind, too wise to be mistaken, and when we cannot trace
his hand, we can always trust his heart." I am chosen — and special. I
want to stand the test well — gracefully, as I have termed it.
I was asked today, "Are they going to put you in the hospital when they
start your treatment (chemo)?"
"Is it really that bad?" I thought to myself, and fear crept in. . . .
Dear Jesus, please give me grace and strength to go through losing my hair.
I am afraid of that — not of others' reactions, but of my own fears. My
prayer is that I find something that I can feel comfortable with so when
that day comes, at least I'll have an alternative.
God, are you teaching what's important and what's not?

I had begun journaling on January 7, several days before my biopsy. These
times of purging my heart and mind focused me on the simplicity of relying on
God. Though I couldn't see the future, and at times doubted my future on earth,
those written connections with God reminded me of two life-changing truths.
First of all, I needed to let go of my desire to control my world. Our human craving to know the game plan, to see all the puzzles pieces at once, provides only a
false sense of security.

Why? Because God did not create us to be in control. His hands that formed the expansive universe are the same hands that catch us when we let go and take a leap of faith by choosing to trust Him to be . . . well, to be Him. *God.*

Some of my favorite qualities about God are His faithfulness (He never lets me go), His omniscience (He knows everything), and His sovereignty (He governs and manages every detail of our lives). I'm still amazed to realize that He allowed me to understand those characteristics more deeply during my lowest points.

He asks us to let go of our agendas and our ideal visions for a picture-perfect life so He can work His perfect plan in us. But while He asks us to let go, He, on the other hand, never lets go of us. That is the second truth that journaling helped me keep my sights on.

God hadn't failed me, and He wasn't about to release His hold just because of a problem that looked huge from my vantage point. He is never surprised or caught off guard, not even by cancer, and I kept being reminded that every needle that stuck me went through Him first. I was not alone.

Treatment

During my six weeks of radiation, I went once a day, Monday through Friday. It took longer to change into the gown I had to wear than it took for the treatment.

Radiation was not fun, but was very doable, with little to no side effects. Those six weeks passed very quickly, and then it was time to begin chemotherapy.

As I mentioned, fear of chemo was at the top of my list of emotions. I was terrified.

April 9, 1990

It has been over a month since I felt the need to write. Maybe that's a good sign that time will pass quickly. It always seems to pass quickly when I <u>don't</u> want it to. Hopefully, my chemo will pass quickly. I start one week from today. I am struggling more over this than anything. I am afraid of the unknown. I was not afraid of surgery or radiation, but I fear chemotherapy. I must claim Philippians 4:6 — "Be anxious for nothing" (NKJV) — especially during these days. I figure I'll have my hair three more weeks. I cannot even imagine how I will deal with that. I'm trusting God will "grace" me through that, too! On Wednesday I will have my IV pump put in. I'm real excited about that, too . . . ha. I hate the cold operating room and I'm tired of needles.

Lord, I can only trust that you have allowed this in my life — so you must have a special plan for me in some way. Help me to <u>feel</u> your presence and purpose in all of this. . . . Give me peace for the next few months of my life.

That first day of chemo tears flowed, despite my resolve to keep them at bay. When the precious nurse asked me what in particular I feared, I could barely whisper, "Everything." Unknowns, loss of control, loss of hair, and more unknowns.

Any life-threatening circumstance involves more than the person whose life is on the line, and my husband walked his own journey of questions and fears as our vows of "till death do us part" took on new meaning.

"It was very sobering the day treatment began. When I saw the red substance being pumped into her body that I knew would take her down in a major way, as well as take every hair from her head, I was filled with silence coupled with deep concern."

Those were Ronnie's thoughts. Knowing something of chemotherapy's power from many ministry visits to cancer patients, and thinking of our young sons who needed their mom, he was well aware of the challenges we were up against. I recall his words on the way home from our second trip to M.D. Anderson: "I don't care if you lose your hair, and I don't care if you lose your breast, but I want you around to raise our children."

On our wedding day, December 31, 1976, we had promised to love each other the rest of our lives. And on that love-filled day just over 13 years earlier, we could not foresee this fear-filled day when our love's lifespan would be threatened.

April 28, 1990

It is Saturday. Ronnie and the boys have gone fishing. My mouth is so sore and swollen I can hardly move it. . . . I have made it through one treatment. I was so scared and I hate the feeling it leaves me — no control. . . . I'm sure it's only a matter of days before my hair falls out. I've laughed and said it has destroyed my stomach and now my mouth — the next thing to go is my hair! . . . I hate chemotherapy. I'm so thankful others are praying for me. I really must be learning to take it one day at a time.

That first of six monthly treatments really threw me for a loop, so they reduced the dosage the next time, and I was better able to tolerate it. Chemotherapy patients are sometimes told that each treatment gets worse as you go. However, in my case I think I was better able to tolerate the successive ones. My fear lessened as I came to know what to expect, and through a process we determined which drugs best helped curtail the side effects.

One thing that did worsen each time was my dread of the huge needle in my chest. Although it lasted only a second or two, it was painful. I had a Port-a-Cath placed surgically in my chest where I received the chemo doses intravenously. My drugs included Cytoxan, Adriamycin, and Fluorouracil (or 5FU), a trio known as the FAC regimen.

I usually slept through the first 24–48 hours, after which the side effects hit. Although I never threw up from the chemo, I did experience nausea, fevers, flu-like symptoms, and horrible mouth sores.

As is common with chemo, just about the time you begin to feel "normal" and the side effects are residing, it's time for another treatment. I remember crying all morning once, anticipating my scheduled appointment that afternoon. But when I arrived at the clinic, my blood levels were too low for me to handle that month's treatment. So I cried the rest of the day because it only meant a delay in the time when it would all be over!

White blood counts determined the timing each month for the treatments. If my count was too low, treatment was postponed for several days. At that time, Nupigen (a drug that stimulates white blood cell production) injections were not available, so my body was on its own to rebuild its immune system.

So the hours and days progressed, sometimes dragging, other times flying by. Each moment became part of a bigger picture God alone could see in whole, a picture I was learning to release my hold on in ever-new ways and rely on God's provision to see me through. It was a time of deep uncertainty and deep faith.

Fortunately, God's grace delved deeper than all of it.

THREE *Highs and Lows*

When I am filled with cares, Your comfort brings me joy.
PSALM 94:19; HCS

Mother's Day

Among the low times that year, Mother's Day stands out like none other. The let-downs actually began the week leading up to it, which included both my birthday and Josh's.

Any parent can relate to wanting to be there, available and whole, for the big events in our children's lives. While birthdays do come around once a year, they *only* come around once a year, and each one marks a significant milestone for a child.

With all the upheaval in our lives, we wanted to make Josh's day extra special, so we planned a big sleepover and pizza party. However, I was so sick that we ended up canceling the sleepover, and Ronnie asked Buster Pray, a friend and one of our staff members at the time to come over to help with the boys and the pizza. I felt terrible, but kept going.

Then to top it off, Nick came down with strep throat, and I had to let others care for him. Because of my low immunity, I spent most of Mother's Day weekend at another staff member's home to keep away from the germs. Bert Miller and his wife, Wanda, were good friends and I was grateful for their hospitality, but I couldn't escape the sadness of not being able to do my job as a mom or enjoying Mother's Day weekend and that special time in my child's life. The hours dragged by that weekend, and I thought I would lose my mind.

More than any other time during this journey, that week nearly did me in. By Sunday -- Mother's Day -- I had nothing left to go on, and the irony felt sickening. Of all days I couldn't be there for either of my children, why did it have to be *that* one? It was a tough reality check that I really was dealing with cancer as a mother with two young sons. My weakened and nauseous condition left me with little strength to process the emotions productively. It was the final straw.

"No more chemo for me," I said. I'd had enough. Perspective was out the window, and that weekend I let Ronnie know it. So much for walking through this gracefully!

Ronnie remembers that day as being a particularly low point, too. "I picked her up off of the floor due to her being so weak. . . . That day it became apparent that we were in a deep challenge."

On the other end of the spectrum, God sent many hugs my way through other people. I can't begin to thank (or even count!) each person who offered encouragements, prayers, helping hands, and smiles through it all. Gifts sent straight from heaven.

One such gift arrived in the midst of a time I dreaded most — shopping for a wig.

I need to backtrack a bit to before chemotherapy began. I had wanted to be prepared and have a wig ready and waiting before my hair started thinning. My goal was to find something that resembled my own hair as much as possible.

After one unsuccessful shopping trip that ended in tears (and no wig), our friends J. B. and Johnelle Hunt stepped in with timely generosity. Soon after I had been diagnosed, Johnelle told me, "I'll do anything you need me to do." Well, she put her words into action when she called around and learned of a place at the Arlington Cancer Research Center in Arlington, Texas, that designed wigs specifically for chemotherapy patients. She and J. B. arranged for me to fly there and back in one day. All I had to do was get on the plane and pick out a wig. Knowing I needed support and extra input, Ronnie and my friend Debby Thompson made the trip with me.

> *February 23, 1990*
> *It has been a dreaded day, but one I know I have to face. Hopefully, when this day is over, I'll feel better (?). . . . I know Ronnie hurts for me. Lord, give us both grace to go thru this.*

Well, that "dreaded" day didn't start out too great. I worried how I would do. I worried how Ronnie would do. I was so thankful for Debby's supportive presence for both of us. And Johnelle? I knew she was a very busy woman, so her sacrifice of time and her concern for me as a woman searching for a wig blessed me hugely that day as I recalled her promise.

God proved faithful once more by helping me joke and laugh. The woman at the wig shop was kind and let me know my only problem was too much gray. Ha! She helped me find a wig I felt good about, plus some turbans I liked and fake bangs to wear under them. And I determined then and there that, of all times warranting some new earrings, this one led the list! All in all, it was a good trip, though I was happy to have it behind me.

There are times in any spiritually minded person's life when it's impossible to deny knowing God showed up in a very direct answer to prayer. Little did I know as I debarked the plane back home in Arkansas that He wasn't done making His presence clear to me.

His biggest sign that He was working arrived at my home while we were still in Texas. We returned to find brownies in the mailbox.

Granted, this discovery might seem insignificant in and of itself, but its meaning spoke volumes to my shaky emotions. Those goodies served as visual (and tasty!) proof that God saw me and remained on call 24/7, even to the point of cluing others in to my needs.

I should have known someone, specifically my friend Vickie White, was praying for me. It's just like God to place us on others' hearts with a supernatural burden to pray. My precious friend didn't even know about my trip or its purpose. She just felt in her spirit that I needed God's help, and she acted in faith that God would be there for me.

Thank you, Lord, for that special blessing. May I be that for someone else someday. What precious lessons you are teaching me thru friends. . . . Thank you for the opportunity to live.

In all my years of trusting in God, it shouldn't surprise me that He sends such personal messages on our behalf. But He never ceases to amaze me. And He doesn't do this only for me; He sees and hears every heart's cry from every one of the billions of people He looks after on earth. All we have to do is watch for Him to show himself and trust that He will.

> *My Presence will go with you, and I will give you rest.*
> *Exodus 33:14; NIV*

Freeing Faith

Trust is a word that sounds good, but putting it into practice can seem quite a bit trickier. When we feel our backs up against a wall and we can't find, plead, demand, or coerce our way to a guaranteed conclusion, it's easy to become cynical. But from my first knowledge of my illness, I determined that I didn't want the poisons of bitterness and envy to take root in me. After all, I had enough poison flowing through my system from the chemo chemicals.

> *May 4, 1990*
> *What a week! This was supposed to have been my good week. . . . My*
> *mouth broke out in sores. Boy, does that hurt. By Saturday my jaw was*
> *swollen. . . . By Tuesday I was running a fever, and not only did my jaw*

hurt but it felt like I had strep throat. I had to go to the ER — what a trip. No makeup, stuck my wig on my head, put on a sweat suit, and went. I didn't even care, I felt so bad. . . . My white blood cell count was down to 0.8. I am supposed to take my chemo again on Monday. Who knows. . . . I'm "learning to be content in whatever state I am in" (Phil. 4:11). Who knows what I'll wake up with tomorrow.

Oh yes . . . the hair is going.

May 16, 1990

Today I did it! I had James cut what is left of my hair off. It was the right time — I was ready. The Lord has been gracious to bring me to this point gradually. I wonder if I have "lost my hair gracefully" as I have prayed earlier. . . .

I held on to my hair as long as I could. In those days, it was not as acceptable as it is today to just put on a baseball cap and go. There was still some taboo about being bald, especially if you had cancer. Plus, I didn't want to frighten my young children, so I chose to wear my wig, turbans, and fake bangs. It was an extremely anxious time in my life, which explains why Philippians 4:6 meant so much to me. But actually, once the hair was gone, that anxiety was gone, also. I guess it was, after all, part of the clutter that had to go for God to do His work in me.

In letting God be God, letting Him hold me, and learning to lean on Him more deeply than ever, I found comfort in His provisions for what my family and I needed. I couldn't be everything to them — not then and not now — but I could set an example for my kids to see what trust looks like in practical living. Humbling? Yes. But also so very freeing amidst the highs and lows.

The good times far outweighed the bad ones. I drank in everything from the spiritual to the physical and held on tightly to whatever measure of faith I had each day. Each hour that God carried me through was part of His carefully orchestrated method of drawing me closer to himself. He met me at each low point and lifted me up to a higher place of resting in Him. Many times I couldn't see the purpose, but He sent his peace, through His Word and through caring people. As I saw Him remain true time and again, I realized He was helping me learn along the way.

And then I was reminded once more of His purposes for allowing me to struggle through cancer. A tough learning curve full of questions and doubts? Yes. But one filled with precious growth.

Dana's Story

*I am pleased to tell you about
the miracles and wonders the
Most High God has done for me.*
Daniel 4:2

My name is Dana Tanner. I am a breast
cancer survivor of nine years, two months and six days
as I write this. My story goes like this…
…I found a lump in my right breast as far back as five years
BEFORE I was diagnosed with invasive ductal carninoma breast cancer.
I was very concerned about this lump, as I had lost my beloved grandmother to
breast cancer and a very dear friend at the age of 28 to breast cancer. I had mammogram after mammogram as well as repeated breast smears as later on I began to have
a discharge in the same breast as the lump was in. The mammograms always came
back clear…not a thing…notta, zip, zero. I had these mammograms all the way up
to three months BEFORE I was diagnosed. The doctor said that the lump must be
a fluid-filled cyst and that I also had fibrocystic breast disease. I wanted to trust
my doctor, I NEEDED to trust my doctor. What I didn't know is that if you
are under the age of 50, your milk ducts are still productive and your breast

tissue is very dense and hard to read on a mammogram unless the cancer is on the surface of the breast tissue. Mine wasn't.

The pain in my breast became so severe that I asked for a second opinion. I discovered that an ultrasound should have been done, as it is a state law that if a lump is palpable, even when the lump doesn't show on a mammogram, that an ultrasound must be performed as well. I wasn't aware that ultrasounds were even an option. When I later made mention of this to a radiologist, he said that they had "let me slip through the cracks," so to speak. It was a tough lesson to learn and one that I hope will help others in my same or similar situation.

On Friday, March 13, 1998, I went in to have a biopsy on the lump in my right breast. While I was in recovery, my family and friends were told in no uncertain terms that while the doctor didn't know what the lump was....he was sure that it wasn't cancer — great news and SO what we wanted and needed to hear.

On Sunday, March 15, 1998, I received a call from my nurse saying that they were surprised, but that it WAS cancer. I was asked to come in and discuss options. My nurse very sweetly prayed with me and handed me booklets about my `type" of cancer. I remember a fog....phone calls to "take back" the good news and share the "new" news.

I became involved in a cancer support group that my pastor's wife and my friend, Jeana Floyd, had started because of her experience with cancer. I remember telling her that I had never known a cancer survivor until I met her and some of the others in the group. That was so encouraging to me after being diagnosed.

After also having an MRI, which revealed a tumor in my left breast as well as the margins being unclear in the right breast after the first surgery, I had a second surgery removing the benign tumor in my left breast, a partial mastectomy removing the remaining cancerous tumor in my right breast and another tumor that was undetected during the first surgery, which also was cancerous, along with lymph node dissection.

After receiving a third opinion, four treatments of standard chemotherapy, two stem cell transplants, and radiation were recommended as treatments. Otherwise, I most likely had five or less years to live.

I received four treatments of standard chemotherapy beginning in May of 1998. Because my cancer had spread to five lymph nodes, I also was advised to have two stem cell transplants, using my own stem cells. I was given a brief period of recovery in order to strengthen myself before the first transplant. I began the first stem cell transplant in October of 1998. With the transplantation, I received one high dose of chemotherapy, administered through a Quinton catheter placed in my chest. This therapy was so severe that I would eventually be in the hospital in isolation with a high temperature, severe nausea, diarrhea, pain, complete loss of taste, loss of appetite, missing finger and toe nails, bone aches, low blood counts, STILL bald, and completely neutropenic. The high-dose chemotherapy killed every good and bad cell in my body. It was especially prominent in the rapid-growing cells which sloughed off very quickly, including the lining of my mouth, throat, esophagus, stomach, and intestines. I was on IV meds constantly for the situations above plus other meds to keep me from being infected from my surroundings, even in isolation.

I was scheduled to have the second transplant right away, but because of damage to my bladder and loss of strength and weight, I didn't receive the second transplant until May of 1999. A different drug was used in this high-dose chemotherapy in case the first drug used wasn't effective. I had the same side effects with this one as well.

I never questioned why God chose to allow this to happen to me, not because you shouldn't, but because I figured WHY NOT ME? I have had the priviledge of being able to share the love of my Savior with boldness that I never had before. I've met people that I wouldn't have met otherwise, been places and experienced things that I wouldn't have been in a position to do otherwise.

Jeana Floyd was there for me in every way. She is not just my pastor's wife, but my dear friend. I love her.

Cancer is not a journey that I would have chosen, but with the prayers and support of so many, the journey has been sweeter than I could ever have imagined.

My favorite verse throughout my cancer journey was 1 Peter 5:10. It says:

"But may the God of all grace, who called us to His eternal glory by Christ Jesus, after you have suffered a while, perfect, establish, strengthen, and settle you."

part two

THE
LEARNING
CURVE

*Teach us to number our days
carefully so that we may develop
wisdom in our hearts.*
PSALM 90:12; HCS

FOUR *Questioning God*

Be still, and know that I am God.

PSALM 46:10; NIV

A Big God

God can take it. Our questions, that is. He's a big God, bigger than any doubts and concerns we throw at Him. He knows our feeble hearts because He created them. And He knows that for all our best intentions, we all reach our limits sooner or later when stress and disappointments shatter our worlds.

Oftentimes, He lets us reach the end of ourselves precisely to help us learn to live by His strength. We may pride ourselves on being independent and capable beings, but when placed next to our Creator, we are needy souls for sure!

God never intended for us to make it through life on our own. He knows far better than we do just how many dangers lie ahead of us, and He's ready and willing to be everything we need for each challenge.

Although He doesn't enjoy seeing us hurt ·— and indeed has fashioned a grand plan to do away with all pain one day — He uses each tear for our benefit, if we'll only let go and cling to Him while He polishes our rough edges.

His greatest goals for us are to worship Him and reflect His loving nature. However, getting even a willing human being to that place of intimate relationship with Him inevitably involves some growing pains. Because we don't like to hurt, and because we like to think we know best, it's easy to start questioning His methods when they're not as comfy as we'd prefer.

Overall, the majority of the time I felt hope and peace and especially God's grace. I felt Him helping me avoid bitterness and resentment, a huge answer to my prayers. Mostly I did not feel anger toward Him for my cancer, but I did experience my share of questions regarding His purposes in my life, as a child would question a parent.

Sometimes the greatest pain in our lives brings about the greatest question marks. There were occasions when doubts crept in and rattled my resolve to rest in His grace. Those were the stretching points when I witnessed the end of my own resources.

I shared already about my first chemo treatment, and looking back once more to those days leading up to it, I'm flooded anew with memories of confusion and disappointment when my situation seemed too much to handle and God said *no* when I expected *yes*.

April 15, 1990 (Easter Sunday)
Tomorrow I take my first chemotherapy treatment. It has been a tough week. My Port-a-Cath did not stay in place, and I had to undergo a second surgery to place it. I do not understand the purpose of that, and it has been "shattering" and "crushing" to my faith. I was so sick after my first surgery, I begged God to make sure it was in place — to even <u>move</u> it if need be. I asked before and truly believed that He <u>could</u> and <u>would</u> answer my prayer! I don't remember ever trusting Him so completely and being so shattered. Why did I have to go thru that again? I have been mad at the Lord. I've wondered, "If He won't answer my prayer in this, where will I be during chemo? What happens when the time comes to lose my hair and I can't feel His presence?"
I feel abandoned.
What purpose could there have been in this week's outcome? It has turned out much different than I thought.

Today has been a special day in the Lord's house. I confessed my anger to the Lord and asked for my broken heart to be healed. I have such fear about tomorrow. My emotions have been wreaked with dread, fear, and pain this week. . . . This has been the hardest week so far — I feel <u>bruised</u> and <u>crushed</u>. Will I stand the test in the coming weeks — gracefully — as I have prayed? My faith is wavering but not gone — after all, I still only have <u>Him</u> to trust in to get me through this. . . . I almost felt God was trying to see how <u>hard</u> it could be. I would never allow my child to hurt this way — especially if I could control <u>all</u> circumstances. My love is human and finite and God's love is superhuman and infinite. I must remember that. My thoughts and feelings are hurt and confused and frightened.... At this point, all I can do is trust, after all. He did get me through this past week. I will still claim Philippians 4 and other Scriptures that have become so important and personal to me.

God give me courage to face tomorrow.

A Matter of Perspective

I did not enjoy being thrust into such a vulnerable spot. *Nothing* seemed to be in my control anymore. Well, nothing except my responses. And I'll admit there were times when my responses weren't exactly what God may have wanted from me. But still, He didn't abandon me. He didn't reject me or my questions. He patiently listened while I cried out to Him, and then He always answered back. Sooner or later, His quiet voice whispered through my anxieties, letting me know He was still with me. I was not in control, but He was. And, oh, what a good thing that was! What a warm place I found right in the center of His arms.

He is not thrown off by your questions, either.

> *When doubts filled my mind, your comfort gave me renewed hope and cheer.*
> *Psalm 94:19; NLT*

However, He is pleased when we ask our questions from a perspective of wanting to know Him better. He wants us to acknowledge that He is still God, and we are still reliant upon Him for everything, right down to the oxygen that flows through our bodies.

Earlier, I wrote of fear — mine and my family's fears. There are two kinds of fear, both of which often leave us asking lots of questions. The difference is one kind of fear is negative, the other positive. Fear that traps us and paralyzes our faith in God is negative, but respectful fear of God is positive.

When someone who seeks God has a healthy fear of Him, that fear causes the person to surrender to His bigness, His holiness, and His right to call the shots. It says, "Yep, I need Him. I can't make it on my own, and it's a good thing He loves me, because otherwise I'd *really* have something to be afraid of."

When we go to Him with our questions, and a humble acknowledgment that He has the authority to do whatever He knows is best for us, He is more than happy to hear us out.

Jesus spent hours listening and responding to questions posed by people who wanted to know Him better. You may know the story of Mary and Martha, two sisters who had just lost their brother, Lazarus. Close friends of Jesus, they had sent for Him when they knew Lazarus was dying. But instead of going right away to the grieving sisters, Jesus delayed His departure, arriving at their home days after Lazarus had been buried.

Naturally, the sisters had questions. How could Jesus let them suffer so much when He easily could have saved their brother? What kind of friend acts so casual about something so tragic?

Martha met Jesus as He approached the house: "'Lord,' Martha said to Jesus, 'if you had been here, my brother would not have died. But I know that even now God will give you whatever you ask'" (John 11:21–22; NLT).

Notice the surrender in her voice? She knew God was still in control, despite the fact that Jesus' actions left her with questions. She knew Him well enough to know that above all He was in control, and being God, He had authority.

Jesus didn't condemn her questions. He had a bigger lesson in mind for her. Yes, she knew He could heal Lazarus, but He wanted her to see that He could even bring Lazarus to life again — which He did (verses 43–44).

In contrast, religious leaders known as Pharisees and Sadducees were jealous of Jesus' authority and constantly attempted to undermine Him (Luke 20). Jesus saw right through His enemies' motivations when they asked questions to trap Him (Luke 20:23).

Just as Jesus had new things to teach Mary and Martha (and you and me!) about himself, He has more to show you through whatever you're dealing with. You may be in the middle of your own cancer battle, or you may be grieving as you watch a loved one endure radiation or chemotherapy. Or, your pain may be from an entirely different source.

Whatever the case may be, know that God is okay with your honest questions when they come from a heart that wants to see Him work in His way.

> *I am still confident of this: I will see the goodness of the LORD in the land of the living. Wait for the LORD; be strong and take heart and wait for the LORD.*
> *Psalm 27:13–14; NIV*

FIVE *Unexpected Treasures*

A cheerful look brings joy to the heart, and good news gives health to the bones.
PROVERBS 15:30; NIV

The Flip Side of Giving

The old saying "It is more blessed to give than to receive" actually came straight from the Bible, spoken by Jesus himself (Acts 20:35; NIV). As someone in ministry, I understand the blessings I receive from giving because I am accustomed to being a giver of my time and other resources.

But God took me on another learning curve through cancer that involved being a taker. In the course of any lifetime, we all find ourselves playing the roles of giver and taker, and it's important to learn to do both well. God had in mind for me to practice being the recipient of other people's resources. And how I needed others back in 1990!

As humbling as it was not being able to handle my daily routine like I was accustomed to, it was refreshing to be handed countless opportunities to watch others live out Acts 20:35. Our friends, our church, our family — all were ready and willing to offer whatever we needed.

Our extended family offered many prayers and a lot of concern. I am sure it was beyond painful for our families to not be able to be with us physically during this time. But because they lived far away, we learned to rely on our church family and close friends in ways we never had before, which deepened and strengthened those relationships as nothing else could.

Where do I begin to describe the ways people encouraged me? From prayers and sharing Bible verses, to meals and childcare, to lunch dates and reassurances about my wig — so many people showed their concern.

Being a safe person for a hurting person is truly an art. It's easy to toss out glib phrases such as "I know how you feel" or "Everything will be okay." But to really walk with someone the entire way along a tough road is not for the weak hearted. There were many people who got down in the mire with my family and me and stuck it out for the long haul.

On that difficult Easter Sunday before chemo began, my friend Debby understood my questions and shared them with me. She didn't criticize or belittle my doubts; in fact, she said she walked through those same feelings and questioned the power of her own prayer life. Other friends shared many Bible verses with me that became anchors for my faith. And several friends who knew the dread I'd felt over losing my hair threw me a surprise birthday party just after my final haircut.

My friend Teenie Moore became like a second mother to me — a role I cherished because my own mother lived too far away to come at a moment's notice. Teenie would show up at my back door and tell me she had come to do "a little ironing." In the beginning, I was too sick to visit with her, but she would stay in the laundry room and do laundry and iron while I was in bed. After I began to tolerate my treatments better, I would sit on the floor at her feet and we'd visit while she ironed my clothes. She also made the best chicken spaghetti and would bring that from time to time. In fact, I still use her recipe!

She and her husband, Louie, took me to the emergency room once after my first treatment when Ronnie wasn't able to, when my blood count was extremely low and I was running a fever. I was quite the sight that day in my wig, sweat suit, and no makeup. Louie rolled me into the emergency room in a wheelchair. Quite humiliating! But what would I have done without them?

A true servant, Teenie changed the sheets on my bed and cleaned out the refrigerator — things you'd let only your mom do for you. I knew my parents ached for me but were unable to make the trip very often, so Teenie's presence must have been comforting to them on some level.

Sometimes spiritual giants come in the forms of everyday folks who hang on gently yet tenaciously to whatever thread of faith is available. God surrounded me with those types of "giants." When I cried, they cried with me. When I rejoiced, they shared my joy. And sometimes they even set me straight when my perspective needed a little boost.

As Frances J. Roberts wrote in *Come Away My Beloved*, "Surely He has given you ministering angels, who may sometimes come to you in the form of your friends. Accept their help as from God, and your blessings will be doubled. You may also, in turn, be used in similar manner to bless others."[1]

Through those angels in disguise, I learned that real-life crises call for real-life heroes, otherwise known as committed friends and family. It's not so much a matter of coming up with the perfect words of sympathy or knowing exactly what someone needs every minute, but rather just being quietly available for whatever needs arise.

That's the model Jesus set for us. He didn't expect His friends and family to have it all together. He spent time with countless people whose faith wavered, who questioned and doubted, and who had little to nothing to offer Him in return. And in the process, He showed people what love looks like.

1 Frances J. Roberts, *Come Away My Beloved* (Uhrichsville, OH: Barbour Publishing, 2004), p. 22.

Treasures of Gold

As I said already, the good times outweighed the bad. God has a way of sending just the right people and pick-me-ups at the moments we need them most. They are treasures worth gold.

My sons' school teachers and their friends' parents often insulated Josh and Nick while Ronnie and I did our best to balance our home life. They made sure Ronnie and I didn't miss any important events on the calendar, and one mother even made sure our kids were on the same baseball team so she could provide backup transportation to practices and games. Through practical help and prayer support, caring people from school and church went beyond the call of duty to help us keep life as normal as possible for the boys.

God knew I'd struggle and be unable to fully take care of my boys at times, but He still had their well-being in hand. Not only was He faithful to see our family through the day-to-day challenges, but He

also reminded me that He had my children's eternal well-being covered as well.

Cancer does not care about age; it hits anyone at any time. But God, who is so much greater than cancer, is deeply attentive to all ages as well. He holds the little ones close in very special ways, which He showed me through the ways He provided for Josh and Nick. In the process of providing for their needs, my Heavenly Father comforted my mother heart too.

August 19, 1990
Tomorrow I begin my last chemotherapy treatment. . . . I can't believe it's almost over. One more boost and one more surgery to remove my catheter. Praise God! I can't even describe how I feel. . . .Today is now Thursday, the day my pump comes off — never to return, hopefully! I cannot wait. The time has passed fairly quickly. I have tried to stay busy.

Another treasure I unearthed during cancer was the simple joy of being healthy and whole. It's easy to take for granted having ten fingers and ten toes, fully functioning arms and legs, a stable mind, a strong heart, and pain-free days (not to mention a full head of hair).

I remember one time coming to a stop sign next to another vehicle. The woman driving that car probably didn't notice me because she was fixing her hair and touching up her makeup. I laughed and thought, *She has hair and she doesn't even realize it.* The gift I received was in the humor of the situation. Then there was the football game when I had to hold my wig on so it wouldn't blow away in the wind! I could either laugh or cry, and I'm grateful God gave me laughter to get me through moments like those when I could have felt resentment.

God stacked those treasured moments one on top of the next until the year passed and we anticipated the holidays again.

> *November 26, 1990*
> *It's a month until Christmas now. The hurry and scurry will now begin.*
> *I'm enjoying this Christmas as though it were my last.*

Ahh, Christmas! Always a time to treasure, but that year held special meaning as I rejoiced to be done with cancer treatment.

Yet God was not done showing me that His work continued. There was much left to process about His mysterious ways, and as I prepared to celebrate the birthday of Jesus — the Light of the world -- I would continue to see God in a fresh light.

SIX *God in a Fresh Light*

The Lord is my rock, my fortress, and my Savior; my God is my rock, in whom I find protection. He is my shield, the power that saves me, and my place of safety.

2 SAMUEL 22:2–3; NLT

Pain Is Pain Is Pain

There are worse things than cancer, and there always will be someone in worse circumstances than our own. Although none of us likes to think about it, the world is full of pain. From the stick of a chemo needle, to the tears of a neglected child across town, to the cries of a mother across the globe who lost her son in a war-torn country, we cannot escape hurts. They are part of life.

God didn't intend for us to suffer. He created an idyllic environment for us in the Garden of Eden. But because of our humanness and Satan's desire to destroy our connection with God, pain and suffering have become a part of living on earth. Health problems, natural disasters, evil at the hands of wicked people — they're all negative effects of an imperfect world.

Right now, God is holding Satan at bay, keeping him from having complete rule over the earth. And someday God will conquer evil and do away with all pain forever, at least for those who choose to follow Him. But for now, we must deal with circumstances that don't always make sense to us and situations that hurt us and those we care about. And while we know this, the reality of pain can be tough to accept when we're in the midst of hard times and we wish God would hurry up and make things right to our way of thinking.

But as 2 Peter 3:9 says, "The Lord is not slow in keeping his promise, as some understand slowness. He is patient with you, not wanting anyone to perish, but everyone to come to repentance" (NIV). God is allowing evil and pain in the world for the time being in order to give more people time to turn to Him and acknowledge their need for Him. His patience shows His grace.

When we're hurting, one of our first responses is to look for some explanation. We want to put logic and reason to something that doesn't make sense to our limited understanding. Why did this happen to us? Could I have done something to prevent it?

Sometimes we wonder if God is punishing us, and we may doubt His goodness and love, or we might feel as though He stopped looking out for us. But just because you're facing something difficult doesn't mean God is turning an angry hand on you. He does, however, want to help you know Him better through your circumstances.

The thing is, we don't give God a chance to show us His perspective if we let our pain drive a wedge between Him and us. He may not choose to tell us all the *whys* in this lifetime; He may just ask us to trust Him and leave some things unanswered for now.

If that seems uncaring, know that He promises to be with you always. He promises *the* comfort of His presence and His strength to get you through whatever He allows. "I will *not* leave you comfortless: I will come to you" (John 14:18; KJV).

But none of us can truly experience the depth of who He longs to be for us unless we turn *to* Him instead of *away* from Him.

The Answer to Pain

Our hurts are no surprise to God. The verses Ronnie carried on a note card remind me that suffering isn't an *if*, but a *when*. At some point we all face our own unique set of struggles. So what's our hope for surviving life on earth?

Our hope lies in God. He does not promise a problem-free existence, but He does promise to be with us all the way:

> *"Do not fear, for I have redeemed you; I have called you by your name;*
> *you are Mine. I will be with you when you pass through the waters, and*

[when you pass] through the rivers, they will not overwhelm you. You will not be scorched when you walk through the fire, and the flame will not burn you. For I [am] the LORD your God, the Holy One of Israel, and your Savior" (Isa. 43:1–3; HCS).

To whom does He promise this? To those who belong to Him, whom He has freed from the fear of eternal death through the death of His Son, Jesus.

I don't know about you, but those verses draw a sigh of relief from me. I am His. I belong to *God* — the all-wise, loving Creator of the universe who calls me by name. If that doesn't inspire awe, I don't know what does.

Just as He saw and felt every needle stick, every wave of nausea, every mouth sore, and every hair that fell from my head, He sees you. He knows exactly what you're dealing with. And believe me, He knows pain. God himself came to earth as a human man named Jesus and died a horrible death for each one of us. And what's really sobering is that if I were the only person on earth, my sins would have drawn enough compassion and love from God to cause Him to come to earth just to save me. It's the same for you. He would have done it for only one of us.

Without Jesus' death, all of us would face an eternity of suffering beyond anything we could imagine on earth. But for each person who chooses to accept that Jesus paid the price we owed for our sin, God promises

an eternal future with Him. Long ago, Jesus was the answer to our sin problem, and He still is the answer to our deepest needs in this lifetime and beyond.

When you hurt, He "comforts [you] in all [your] troubles" (2 Cor. 1:4; NIV). He calls himself "your healer" (Exod. 15:26) and "your Savior" (Isa. 43:3).

Pain is pain is pain, whatever unique form it takes in your life. But God always, always will be God. His character never changes (Mal. 3:6), and He offers himself to you very personally right now:

> **When you fear the future, He whispers,** *"I know the plans I have for you . . . plans to prosper you and not to harm you, plans to give you hope and a future" (Jer. 29:11; NIV).*
>
> **When worries keep you awake,** *"He grants sleep to those he loves" (Ps. 127:2; NIV).*
>
> **When you feel alone, He promises,** *"I will never leave you nor forsake you" (Heb. 13:5; NKJV).*
>
> **When you wake up dreading the day ahead,** *He will "satisfy [you] in the morning with [His] unfailing love, that [you] may sing for joy and be glad all [your] days (Ps. 90:14; NIV).*
>
> **When you need a friend, He says to you,** *"My presence will go with you, and I will give you rest" (Exod. 33:14; NIV).*

When you can't go on, He whispers, *"My grace is sufficient for you, for My strength is made perfect in weakness"* (2 Cor. 12:9; NKJV).
When you don't know where to turn and you need a dose of joy, you can pray to Him, *"Show me the path of life; in Your presence is fullness of joy; at Your right hand are pleasures forevermore"* (Ps. 16:11; NKJV).

Part of the learning curve God took me on during my cancer days was to show me more than ever before that life begins and ends with Him. When my faith was tested, it survived (and even thrived) because my foundation was Jesus Christ. There's no way I got through that on my own. He showed up with fresh grace each day, even on the days I didn't feel like showing up! And He wants to do the same for you.

Healing Defined

"Okay," you say, "that might be easy for you to say because He *healed* you. He doesn't do that for everyone. How do I know He'll do the same for me?"

A valid question.

He did heal me, and I did not have to lose my breast. I am forever grateful for that gift. It's true that He allowed me to raise my boys and enjoy many full, cancer-free years and counting.

It's also true that God does not always answer our prayers like we want Him to. Many people lose their battles with cancer, just like many children grow up unloved, many wars do not cease, and many relationships fall apart.

God calls himself our healer, but how do we reconcile that statement with the very real fact that sometimes He doesn't heal? In order to come to terms with that question, we need to understand His bigger definition of healing.

November 26, 1990
Julia was saved and baptized last night.

When we pray for healing, we most often want healing in this lifetime. Less than a month after I wrote that November sentence in my journal, God reminded me that His idea of healing isn't always the same as ours.

December 13, 1990
Today I go back for my three-month checkup. Yesterday, Julia and I and several other friends went out for lunch. We were supposed to celebrate all being through (with our treatments), but Julia has a spot on her spine. I guess chemo doesn't take care of "everything" after all. I am afraid for her.
December 14, 1990

Julia did not get a good report yesterday. The cancer is all in her spine.
They said her prognosis is not good — maybe one year. God, why? I
do not understand. I hate this disease called cancer. God, I feel so empty
— so helpless — so hopeless — so nothing. I feel so stunned.
How do I pray? What do I say? Julia's world came to a halt yesterday, but
life still marches right on. It seems so cruel. How can this be? . . .
I guess it's not whether you live or die, but if God will be most glorified. Help
Julia to be totally bathed in your love. Give her that special peace that only
you can give. Disperse that grace that you pour on when we need it. May all
of Julia's family come to know you. Work a miracle.

Complete healing from a human perspective means being cured from all sickness, free to go on with a full life on earth. Yet God's idea of complete healing is grander in scope.

The truth is, all of our bodies are temporary. He healed me of cancer, but my body is still made only for earth, just as my friend's was. My complete healing will come someday when Jesus welcomes me to eternity with Him. Take a look at what 1 Corinthians 15:50–57 (NLT) says:

Our physical bodies cannot inherit the Kingdom of God. These dying bodies
cannot inherit what will last forever. But let me reveal to you a wonderful
secret. We will not all die, but we will all be transformed! It will happen

in a moment, in the blink of an eye, when the last trumpet is blown. For when the trumpet sounds, those who have died will be raised to live forever. And we who are living will also be transformed. For our dying bodies must be transformed into bodies that will never die; our mortal bodies must be transformed into immortal bodies. Then, when our dying bodies have been transformed into bodies that will never die, this Scripture will be fulfilled: "Death is swallowed up in victory. O death, where is your victory? O death, where is your sting?" For sin is the sting that results in death. . . . But thank God! He gives us victory over sin and death through our Lord Jesus Christ.

It's difficult for us to comprehend how complete healing comes only *after* an earthly death (for those who belong to God). We still face sorrow when a loved one passes away, and if we're the ones facing the end of life on earth, we still feel deep emotions about leaving behind those we love. We feel like we'll miss out on cherished memories that will never be and dreams that will never become reality. But God offers us something wonderful that lasts far longer than our decades in this life. He offers us *hope* and *forever* with Him that this world can't hold a candle to. That is reason for celebration amidst any uncertainty.

This life isn't all there is. In fact, it's barely a glimpse of the abundant life God has waiting in the wings for those who give their hearts to Him and accept

His gift of salvation. For those folks, death has no lasting power. It has lost its sting.

An eternal perspective of healing can provide an enormous amount of relief and comfort during dark days of cancer or any other circumstance that threatens to derail your joy. Take comfort in that truth today, and hang on to God. He will show you His faithfulness in very personal ways.

After Julia's death, I was reminded again of the fragility of life and that we're not promised a carefree journey. There's no guarantee I won't face cancer again. I thought a lot about that after my treatments ended. As long as I was having surgery or going for treatments, I felt I was fighting it. But especially when someone I knew died from cancer, I wondered, *Now who's fighting mine?*

More questions, more uncertainties. But one thing I could take comfort in — Julia made her decision to turn to God before it was too late. She accepted that she needed His gift of salvation.

Because of that, she has been with her personal Savior ever since she breathed her last breath, experiencing complete freedom from pain as well as unfathomable joy she never knew on earth.

That is God's guarantee.

SEVEN *Better for It*

*I will bow down toward your holy temple and will praise your name for your love and
your faithfulness, for you have exalted above all things your name and your word.
When I called, you answered me; you made me bold and stouthearted.*

PSALM 138:2−3; NIV

Changed

As this book is in process, the 2006 Christmas season is in full swing. I have
anticipated sharing my cancer journey for years now, and these weeks of delv-
ing into the past have been a journey in their own right. God has brought me a
long way from the tumultuous months of 1990. Although the emotions aren't as
acute, nor are the fears and uncertainties of nearly two decades ago, I have relived
those days to some degree as this book takes shape. I remember Christmas 1990,
mere months after completing chemotherapy. I felt such a new lease on life, a new

appreciation for the gift of hope. Hope meant more to me that Christmas than ever before, and I pray I would never lose the lessons and growth God so mercifully taught me through cancer.

One of the great misfortunes of any tragedy is coming away from it unchanged for the better. When God allows a crisis in anyone's life, He intends to bring good from it.

Romans 8:28 embodies the hope God's followers have in Him in any situation: "We know that in all things God works for the good of those who love him, who have been called according to his purpose" (NIV).

Did you catch that three-letter word *all?* There isn't a single experience or a stitch of pain that God ignores. He wants to use everything for your good if you love Him. When I think of some of the Bible's "greats" — real people who trusted God through the good and bad times —I'm inspired to trust Him all the more with my own concerns.

One biblical hero of faith who comes to mind is Joseph from the Old Testament. You can find his story in Genesis 37, 39–50. God had amazing plans for His chosen people of Israel, and He chose Joseph to play a vital role in preserving that entire nation.

Joseph had everything going for him. He was charming, attractive, and wealthy — not to mention he was his father's favored son. But his jealous older brothers sold him into slavery and he ended up in the foreign land of Egypt. From

there, Joseph's road continued full of potholes and bumps along the way. Even though he went from riches to rags, he rose to prominence as a servant of the captain of the palace guard. Unfortunately, the captain's wife wrongly accused him of attacking her, which landed him in jail. However, Joseph remained faithful, and while in jail he again earned the respect of his superiors and eventually the pharaoh. When he was transferred to the pharaoh's palace, he became the second most powerful leader in the land — a perfect position to help his brothers, who unwittingly arrived on his doorstep asking for aid for their people during a severe famine.

Did you catch all that?

This up-and-down life story would have most of us hanging from an emotional string, wondering when the scissors would snip and we'd take our last tumble. From a human standpoint, there's no reason why the man should have had any hope for a better life. But Joseph did not look at things from a human standpoint. Joseph allowed God to show himself strong, and undoubtedly was changed for the better.

I can only think that his many years of suffering provided Joseph with a lot of opportunity to work through grief, self-pity, disappointment, humiliation, loss of dreams, loss of control, resentment, anger, doubts about God's goodness . . . and ultimately godly character growth. Genesis 50:20 records his attitude about his brothers' betrayal, the spark that ignited the fire that burned him over and over: "You intended to harm me, but God intended it for good to accomplish what is now being done, the saving of many lives" (NIV).

Joseph looked for God's hand in his circumstances, and God showed up each time, though probably not usually in Joseph's time frame. Surely Joseph would not have chosen slavery, unjust accusations, and prison. But he did choose to keep trusting God, and God blessed him and many others as a result.

You and I often don't have control over the things that happen to us, but we always have a choice to keep looking to God to see us through. Sometimes the greatest brokenness in our lives brings about the greatest growth and a closer relationship with the Lord. He wants to bring you good even in your darkest hours, when life feels bleak and hope seems to mock your hurts.

Stronger through Brokenness

January 3, 1991
1990 has come and gone now. What a year! One that has forever changed my life. On most days I look back at the year with gratefulness — that it's

over (ha!) and that I lived through cancer and treatment. God taught me
many things and I am no longer content with an ordinary walk with God.
I desire to walk more closely and to be used more by Him. I have been
changed. My fear is a return to mediocrity –– it's so easy to be caught up
in "things," and before you know it, your perspective is warped.

On some days, I fear reoccurrence of cancer. It seems to lurk out at me
everywhere. . . . Many days are frustrating. "Some trust in chariots, and
some in horses; But [I] will remember the name of the Lord [my] God"
(Ps. 20:7; NKJV). I must continue to stay grounded in this verse and not
let fear of the future overcome me.

Next week Ronnie goes to the staff retreat — when I began this journal
one year ago. I felt then, Lord, you were working in my heart and prepar-
ing me for something special and exciting in my life. Little did I know. . . .
Father, do what you want to do in my life in 1991.

My spiritual life had basically been steady and consistent up until my biopsy revealed a malignant lump. My faith had been tested previously, but never to the extent that it was stretched through cancer. Cancer put God's Word to the test, and God's Word stood up every time. Faith in my life now means:

1. being totally, helplessly dependent on God;
2. trusting Him when things are beyond my control;

3. knowing He is in control and I'm not;

4. trusting Him when I'm afraid;

5. trusting Him for the future and the unknown;

6. knowing I will spend eternity with Him because I have placed my total trust in Jesus alone.

When I felt so crushed during spring of 1990, my friend brought me a devotional about being "crushed" and the sweet fragrance chamomile gives when it is bruised and crushed. When we are broken, we can either make ourselves and others more miserable, or we can ask God to help us become better because of it.

Through my suffering, God has given me much mercy and compassion for those who are hurting. He has given me the desire to share with others the compassion He showed to me in the midst of my greatest pain. And He gave me my life's verse, 2 Corinthians 1:3–5, and made it more true-to-life than I expected.

Praise be to the God and Father of our Lord Jesus Christ, the Father of compassion and the God of all comfort, who comforts us in all our troubles, so that we can comfort those in any trouble with the comfort we ourselves have received from God. For just as the sufferings of Christ flow over into our lives, so also through Christ our comfort overflows (NIV).

Ronnie also sees how cancer grew our entire family. "I know God used that in both of our lives and in our family in a major way. So many people have been helped across the country due to Jeana's sickness and our transparency with the church. We did not hold it back, but told folks where we were and what we were facing continually. It has helped our boys remember those days of great faith and know that today, every day is a gift. We believe that God healed her. We know that the Lord let us all go through it for our good."

He also believes that God used that entire experience to truly ignite him to be pastor of our church. He'd served there by position for four years; but through cancer, the Lord knit our hearts into oneness with our congregation.

As for the two of us together, having cancer kept us from taking our marriage for granted — as it does life in general. Cancer focused us on what's important and what isn't. We realize we're not guaranteed the time we think we'll have with each other. It deepened our love when we knew that love could be taken from us.

> *Teach me to do your will, for you are my God; may your good Spirit lead me on level ground.*
> *Psalm 143:10; NIV*

Having cancer also makes you realize how much one day can change your life and that life is fragile. It makes you treasure each day as a gift. I still get overwhelmed at times that I am able to go and breathe and do! I've asked God never to let me forget these lessons.

There's a prayer that says, "Lord, thank you for accepting me as I am, and thank you as well for loving me too much to let me stay the way I am." Growing pains are a sign of life, a sign that God isn't finished with His work in us yet. Although they are not often enjoyable and we rue the pain they cause, they do remind us we're still alive and kicking on this earth. We're still able to influence others with our lives. We're still able to create memories and make a positive difference to those we love. May none of us settle for mediocre relationships with God or other people. That would be a tragedy indeed.

You are alive today, which means God has a plan for you right now. Don't pass up a single precious moment of being alive and in God's hands. It's a safe, always growing place of meaning and hope.

EIGHT *Taking It from Here*

Let all that I am praise the Lord; may I never forget the good things he does for me.
PSALM 103:2; NLT

New Directions

> *October 19, 1993*
>
> *Just for the sake of keeping up with what is now going on in my life, last week was one filled with much "cancer" activity. I did two interviews for TV and then left for Little Rock to participate in the Breast Cancer Summit. I really don't know what direction my life is taking, but I feel like the Lord may be changing my focus or direction. . . . I remain open before the Lord as to what and where He may take me from here. . . .*
>
> *Be my teacher, Father, and give me direction.*

Remember how my cancer story began with a simple request that God would remove the clutter from my life? Well, He answered that prayer and prepared me for a new direction. I've been in ministry a long time, but I never imagined He'd put me in a position to encourage others who are battling cancer.

Many cancer patients are looking for extra support to help them know they're not alone in their illness. Support groups are a common place to search for those answers. But after attending only one, I left feeling desperate for God's truth. I discovered that many groups came up with therapeutic methods that didn't help people find the real answers they needed to cope with their illness. At least back then, one method taught was to visualize Pac-Man eating your cancer! Our world is full of coping mechanisms and versions of truth — many that sound logical and offer some temporary relief. But in the end, they fall short of providing the real answer. There is only one Truth, and His name is Jesus.

There were times I wanted to holler that they were missing the point. People were dying from this disease, and they needed to know about Jesus' offer of eternal salvation before their days on earth came to an end.

My faith spurred me to offer something different. I became so burdened by the need to clarify the source of true hope and healing, that I considered starting my own group. Ronnie encouraged me to do it, but I hesitated for a while. As much as most cancer patients yearn for the support and hope, most have some resistant emotions about going to a group. Becoming so involved in one, not to mention *coordinating* the efforts, meant admitting to the reality of dealing with the disease. It's a huge admission about not wanting to be a victim, a recognition of what's happening. Because many people want to push the truth aside and forget they ever dealt with cancer, getting involved in a group can be humbling and intimidating.

While I experienced some of those emotions, I never wanted to forget cancer happened to me. Doing so would have been a huge spiritual mistake for me, because God used my heartbreak and pain to mold my character to be more like His own. I could not turn my back on the journey He'd brought me through; He allowed it for specific reasons, two of which were so I could enjoy a deeper closeness with Him as well as show His mercy to others in new ways.

As it turned out, I waited a full year after my treatment ended before committing to start a group. I needed that time to recover emotionally before being able to give out again.

The group began with a banquet at our church. I invited a guest speaker who was a cancer survivor, and we advertised it to the community. Approximately 300 people came out for it. From that night, I compiled a mailing list, and the support group was born. The Cancer Network of Northwest Arkansas (CNNA), as our group was known, referred to a "network of caring and sharing Christ." We chose a logo in purple, which I had been told represented hope.

In the beginning, we met every Sunday evening, but switched to monthly meetings when the schedule became too much. Our attendance depended to some extent on when the meetings fit with patients' treatments and side effects. Eventually I settled on meeting for six weeks in a row, followed by a break before resuming our meetings again. This was most effective and we had great response, sometimes with as many as 50 people present.

Our speakers varied from survivors to medical professionals, although I often spoke and led the entire time. I spent countless hours in the early days calling people, ministering to family members, visiting hospitals, and, sad to say, attending funerals.

At that point, my world really did revolve around cancer. My husband even remarked that all my friends had cancer — and there seemed to be some truth in that!

I led the group for about nine years before turning it over to a couple, Mark and Dana Tanner, who'd been faithful volunteers. Dana has her own cancer survival story that is quite miraculous, including two stem-cell transplants. See her story on page 44. Still a dear friend, she is a reminder to me that God is not restricted by medical diagnoses.

One of my focuses during CNNA meetings was to help family and friends of cancer patients learn ways to help their loved ones deal with their illness.

Having cancer affects not only the patient, but family members as well, and even friends, co-workers, and acquaintances. It is not a disease that happens in isolation. Because it is one of the most dreaded and feared sicknesses, each person's response is individualized. We all react differently to our own situation, as well as to the feelings and emotions of those closest to us.

I have observed through the years the incredible stress cancer places on a couple's relationship. Depending on the strength of their relationship, cancer will either strengthen it or possibly bring it to collapse. Rarely did I see it make an already shaky marriage better or weaken a strong one.

One of the main things I realized through my personal experience is that many times the spouse's feelings get neglected. People were always asking how I was doing, but rarely did they consider the emotion and stress Ronnie was under. Because people always asked about me, and Ronnie continually tried to be strong for me, there were times when he needed to be allowed to be weak and vulnerable, times he needed someone to ask how *he* was doing. There he was, trying to be a support to me and to our children, while pastoring a huge church full time. He never missed a chemotherapy treatment and never missed a Sunday preaching. It was a lot to carry. Several of our friends were sensitive to this and met a real need for Ronnie by allowing him to express his own fears and challenges.

I have seen over and over how couples try to be so strong for each other. Couples who truly love one another attempt to protect each other. But both partners need an objective person to share their deepest fears with and not feel they are being weak for his or her loved one. I became that many times for people in my support group. When patients wanted to talk about death and dying, it was very uncomfortable to do so with their spouses without upsetting them. But they could talk to me because I was less emotionally involved. I would let them say whatever they wanted, and I listened when their feelings and courage changed from one conversation to the next. And it is just as crucial for spouses to have people they can be equally as honest with about their own fears.

Another area of great need is for parents of children with cancer. I dealt with very young children as well as young adults in their twenties. I remember one precious young woman in particular. She was only 22 when she died. A true treasure, she accepted the Lord as her Savior during her treatment and went to be with Jesus at such a young age. Having children that age now, I understand more completely the heartache her family must have felt in losing her.

As I previously stated, in dealing with our children about my cancer, we tried to keep them abreast of key events in time for whatever was next in my treatment or stage of the game. Not wanting them to carry any more of the burden than

absolutely necessary, we sheltered them as much as we could. From the many cases I've seen, I believe God graces our children through these times, just as He does us.

I'm amazed by how resilient children can be; they can even bring a sense of lightheartedness to a difficult journey. When my hair started growing back, Josh was growing out his flat-top, so he and I had a race to see whose hair could grow fastest. And one time Nick found my wig in the closet and paraded around the house in it, providing a humorous illustration of how God can lighten a heavy load through the innocence of our children.

I *never* encourage parents to keep their cancer from their children, but I encourage them to use discernment and sensitivity in sharing details according to the age and emotional makeup of the individual child. Obviously in our case, Josh's understanding of "Mom having cancer" was much greater than Nick's due to the age difference. Nick had no clue what it meant to have cancer; all he knew was that Mom was sick. We practiced a learn-as-we-go policy throughout surgery, radiation, and chemotherapy.

Practical Advice for Helping Cancer Patients

Loved ones often need help understanding the roller-coaster emotions cancer patients experience. Since understanding breeds compassion and strength, it's important to allow those patients room to run the gamut of emotions. Here are a few common "rights" I taught in the support group:

Rights and Privileges of a Cancer Patient

To feel one way today and the opposite tomorrow: Feelings come and go, depending on any number of conditions. Days leading up to and following treatment may be particularly rough, or any new experience during treatment may cause anxiety. As much as possible, go with the flow.

To say "I'm finished": As frightening as this can be to hear, it helps to expect a patient to reach this point one or more times throughout treatment. Courage will ebb and flow, so work hard to calm your own nerves and respond with sensitivity.

To think out loud: Some people are more verbal, and others process more inwardly. Allow room for both, but be prepared to listen often.

To express fears: Keep a sensitive eye open to spoken and unspoken clues to fear. Don't push for explanations, but gently encourage a cancer patient to get things out in the open instead of keeping emotions bottled up.

To be involved in decisions, not excluded: Help your loved one feel alive and empowered by keeping them involved in the decision-making process when it comes to their treatment and care. We all need to feel necessary and needful. Unless circumstances make it impossible, avoid going around the patient and making decisions based on what you feel might be best.

To have one or two pity parties: The freedom to fall apart on occasion can go a long way toward purging waves of negative emotions. Let them feel their emotions before encouraging them to bounce back.

To laugh when they feel like it: Life can still be good with cancer! Enjoy the happy moments to their fullest. You're still creating memories together.

To have time alone (with God to sort out feelings): Sometimes having caretakers around can become overwhelming, so give space when space is needed.

To not talk if they don't want to: Again, a little space for quiet time can be rejuvenating

To be loved unconditionally: Let your loved one know you're there for the long haul.

Another practical way you can show you care is by sending encouraging notes with short prayers. Through CNNA, we came up with several standard note cards that expressed brief sentiments. Here are a few to help you get started:

- God brought you to my mind today. . . .
- One of God's promises is that He will never leave us. . . .
- Adversity is when we draw near to God. . . .
- It is my joy to pray for you during this time. . .
- I'm praying this week for the peace of God to be with you. . . .
- I want you to know I am praying for you and your family. . . .

Those last three bring me to my next suggestion. It is one we sometimes don't see as being practical or

hands-on, but from God's point of view it is the most powerful gift we can offer someone in need. It is the gift of prayer. God hears and acts in response to our prayers. In fact, He loves hearing from us.

Whether or not you were a praying person when cancer entered your life, most likely the illness prompted thoughts about spiritual things as you felt your level of peace waver. Here's a simple acrostic I gave to the support group that may develop a habit of turning to God for peace.

How does a cancer patient spell relief? P-E-A-C-E
P — *Pray.*
E –– *Enjoy each day.*
A — *Accept this as "Father filtered."*
C — *Center your thoughts on Him and His will for your life — study His Word, the Bible.*
E — *Expect to see God's hand move in your life during this time.*

These are only a few of the ways you can let someone know you're thinking of him or her. It doesn't take much to lift someone's spirit, so stay alert to how you can be a hug for someone who's hurting. You may not know in this lifetime just how much any small gesture might mean.

Gayla's Story

When I found a lump while taking a shower, I really wasn't concerned but thought I should have it checked out. The doctor was really not concerned. She thought it was just a cyst but made an appointment for a mammogram the next week, as this was the Monday of Thanksgiving week.

After my mammogram, I was told I needed to talk to the doctor. She informed me that we really needed to schedule a biopsy as soon as possible as the lump looked suspicious but told me not to be overly concerned. The biopsy was scheduled on a Friday. Again, I was really not concerned, as I had several friends who had biopsies and the results were negative. I told the doctor it would be fine to call me at work with the results.

Monday morning I received the call that changed my life. The doctor said he had the results of my biopsy and it was determined that the lump was cancer and it was at Stage II. I was in total shock! I had convinced myself I had nothing to worry about.

At this point, I began a journey that I will never forget. I would never ask to take this journey again, but I can say that I am thankful for the journey. What a blessing to be working for Jeana's husband, Dr. Floyd, at the time of my diagnosis. Of course, the Lord knew this already. Not every employer would understand the journey I was about to embark on. Dr. Floyd's first concern was not for himself but for me. What a blessing the Lord had already brought into my life with my co-worker, Joy Porter. She stepped in and took care of Pastor Floyd and my responsibilities so that I did not have to worry about anything but getting well. And what a blessing to have Jeana who had already walked in my footsteps to walk beside me every step of the way and Pastor to understand what Tony, my husband, was going through.

The Lord blessed me with a wonderful Christian surgeon, Dr. John Kendrick. Within a week we had scheduled surgery and I once again looked on the up side, thinking I would have a lumpectomy, radiation, and be done. The lumpectomy was not successful and we scheduled another lumpectomy to no avail. So within three weeks I was scheduling my 3rd surgery. . . a radical mastectomy and reconstruction surgery. The positive side was that my lymph nodes were clear.

Clinically, the following few months were filled with doctor's visits, tubes, needles, chemo, nausea, baldness, and fatigue. Spiritually, the following few months I grew stronger in my faith, stronger in my walk with the Lord and in my prayer life than I had ever been in my life. For the first time in my

Christian life, I fully and totally gave the Lord control of my life. I had such a peace that whatever the outcome of my situation, He was going to take care of my family and me. Tony and I were totally dependent on Him.

My life went on hold and all the things that I thought were so important were not so important. Your priorities totally change. Your perspective on life changes forever.

I really had time to spend hours with the Lord while I lay in bed too sick to get up.

I learned how important it is to call a friend and pray for them when you think of them. One of my church's great prayer warriors, Teenie Moore, called me at least four times a week to pray with me. This woman prayed for and with so many different people, yet she always had time for me. She claimed Bible verses for me with the Lord.

I learned what true sacrificial friendship is because my friend Kathy McClure was beside me at every chemo treatment. She didn't ask if she could go or if I needed her to go, she was just there to hold my hand. She was there with a bag of snacks, magazines, projects to work on, and conversation to take my mind off of what I was doing.

Our church family brought food, called and checked on us, and prayed with us. Our daughter learned the true meaning of a spiritual family. The sisterhood you develop with fellow breast cancer survivors was so important. Sisters that I didn't even know that well would sit with me in the *hospital and at my home following surgery when my husband had to go back to work and Lauren was in school. What a calming thing when there is someone who has already experienced what you are going through. You learn you can ask anything — nothing is off limits. What a blessing.*

My marriage will never be the same. Tony and I learned to appreciate each other and not to take each other for granted. Our relationship is deeper and sweeter because of my experience with cancer.

So, would I ever want to experience cancer again? Definitely not. Has my life been enriched and blessed by the experience? Most definitely yes. My verse claimed by Teenie Moore the day of my first surgery is, "Do not fear, for I am with you; Do not anxiously look about you, for I am your God, I will strengthen you, Surely I will help you, Surely I will uphold you with My righteous right hand" (Isa. 41:10).

part three

A LITTLE EXTRA

*I came that they may have life, and
have it abundantly.*
JOHN 10:10; NASB

Concluding Thoughts

No eye has seen, no ear has heard, no mind has conceived what God has prepared for those who love him.

I CORINTHIANS 2:9; NIV

Remember

> *December 8, 1993*
> *Just returned from Memphis, Tennessee, where I spoke yesterday at Bellevue Baptist Church for their Ladies Ministry. What an opportunity. God is so good to me — can't believe how He has blessed me as a result of my having cancer.*

God has many names for himself that describe His character and role in our lives. Almighty, I AM, Abba, and Jehovah are only a few that embody an aspect of who He is. One personal favorite of mine is Jehovah Rophe, meaning "God is my healer." Ronnie had Rophe put on my personalized car tag, which gave me many opportunities to share what God had done in my life and served as a visual reminder to me of all He brought me through. I know now more than ever that His faithfulness is new every day and it endures for all generations. Because of His faithfulness, we can approach Him, trusting that He isn't some far-off, distant deity who doesn't care what we're going through. His faithfulness isn't limited by time or space or medical probabilities, and it isn't dependent on our perfection.

Like I wrote earlier, God does not waste an ounce of our pain. He wants to transform each hurt into something of beauty that will draw us closer to Him and help us share His love with others who need a dose of it.

Cancer has several long-lasting effects, and I'm not referring to physical ones. Because of cancer, your life will never be the same. With God's help, it will be better. Instead of "getting over" cancer, which will never happen, you will gain a new and deeper value system. You don't have to fear the future. When you leave it in God's hands, your relationship with Him can be more fulfilling and real than you ever imagined.

Time has a way of dulling the edge of pain, a healthy thing in many ways. Once we've dealt with the hurts, we need to move on to the next season of life God has waiting. However, we're also wise to actively keep sight of our areas of growth so we don't take for granted where God has brought us from, and so we hold on to hope for wherever He plans to take us next.

So remember . . .

Some things I remember from my days of chemo:
. . . the fear of the first treatment
. . . Big Red — Adriamycin
. . . red medicine, red fingernails, red Jell-O
. . . potato soup
. . . losing my hair
. . . combing out my hair on the deck at night
. . . Compazine jitters
. . . Ativan
. . . feeling the greatest uncertainty and the greatest peace
. . . the greatest sorrow and the greatest joys
. . . singing "No More Night"
. . . peace in the midst of the storm
. . . rest
. . . timely Scriptures

What does your list of remembrances include?

Awakened by Grace

One thing I won't soon forget is the theme of *grace*. Anyone who witnesses God's grace in a personal way can vouch for its life-changing power. Grace is something we receive that we don't deserve. Salvation, for instance. Our sin makes us unworthy of being acceptable to God. However, Jesus' death on our behalf was the single greatest act of grace the world will ever see. This grace became the theme of my journal as cancer taught me about it in new and profoundly personal ways. I felt God's grace in each Bible verse someone shared with me, in my prayer times with Him, in the large and small gestures of care from others, and in each day I was still around to spend time with my husband and children. God also showed me His grace through His quiet voice reassuring me that He was still in control, that His ways are always better than mine, even when they may not make sense to me.

Grace does not come cheaply for the giver. It cost my friends and loved ones time, money, energy, and emotions each time they gave of themselves on my behalf. And it cost God dearly to offer me eternal life.

I still am in awe of the effects of grace, namely how it shows love in action. It causes me to want to give back.

My deepened experience of God's loving grace made me discontent with giving Him less than my whole self. And that's what God desires from us. He wants us to know His love so completely that we can't help but offer back to Him everything He's given us. God wants all of us. All of me and all of you.

Only when the Lord has access to a whole heart can a person experience the breadth of grace. Let Him sift out the clutter and bring you closer to himself. He guarantees that your only regret will be if you don't lean on Him.

Take a chance today and allow God to awaken His grace in your life. You will experience joy, peace, and healing like you never imagined possible. And you will have the assurance that no matter the outcome of your current struggles, God's healing awaits you.

God wants to bless you and others through your faith in the midst of crisis, whatever form your pain takes. He has joy in store for you today. When you are God's, your future is secure and altogether wonderful.

That's grace.

Grace, peace, hope, and healing to you. . . .

Pat's Story

I'm not always good at remembering dates, but there are certain ones that are so special that they really stick in my mind. I remember the best ones: July 11, 1970, when my best friend, my God-sent other half, my incredibly wonderful husband, John, and I were married; February 24, 1981, when our lives were blessed by the joy-filled birth of our son, Brian; November 27, 1983, when God completed our family with the addition of our very special daughter, Andrea. I also remember another date — September 8, 2000, the day I was diagnosed with breast cancer. Until that day, I had lived a blessed life. Doors had always opened for me: a loving family, good grades in school, a college scholarship, a great husband, good jobs, wonderful children. Even death, when it touched our families, while sad, was timely and not unexpected. On September 8, 2000, life was suddenly not the joyful adventure it had been. I had CANCER. I was stunned. I was weak. I was helpless. I was right where God wanted me to be.

I had always taken pride in being independent. I viewed myself as a self-reliant person, in control of my emotions in public and able to do almost anything I wanted or needed to do: teach myself macramé and needlepoint, learn to snow ski, go through natural childbirth, teach school, manage my husband's office, hook up a four-horse trailer and drive hundreds of miles with my young daughter, change the battery in a car, make homemade biscuits and jam, coach youth sports . . . All of these things meant nothing when I found out I had breast cancer.

I think that the most devastating aspect of the whole experience was losing control of my life. There was absolutely, positively NOTHING I could do to change things. I felt a tremendous sense of weakness in knowing I was helpless and that I could not control the overwhelming emotions that went along with that sense of weakness. When I heard the words "You have beast cancer," I said nothing. I went home, told my husband not to tell anyone (including our children), and went to bed. When we went to church the next day, I did not want anyone to know anything. I knew that I would burst into tears if anyone said anything to me. I could not stand the thought of people feeling sorry for me and seeing my tears.

By Sunday afternoon, my husband John had insisted that we tell our children. They were teenagers, Jesus Christ had blessed them with salvation, and they were mature enough to handle it. Through our son, our friends Steve, who was on staff at our church, and his wife Laura had been told about the cancer. They came by that Sunday afternoon and shared many wonderful words of prayer with John and me. I received the most comfort from Steve's word: It is okay to be weak. That is when you need God the most. I really felt the true meaning of 2 Corinthians 12:9 for the first time.

My husband John is a general surgeon with lots of experience with breast cancer patients. One of his partners was doing the surgery, and a plastic surgeon was doing the reconstruction at the same time. Thankfully, we were able to schedule the surgery quickly. They called us with the pathology report of breast cancer on Saturday, and the surgery was the following week. I had hoped I would be able to have just a lumpectomy, but further tests indicated that a mastectomy was needed. I remember being surprised at how much I really hadn't accepted the fact that I must have a mastectomy until John told me that it was necessary on the morning of the surgery. I was checking into the hospital, and I broke down and really cried right there in public. I had never liked showing that kind of "weakness" in front of people. I can remember feeling that I was watching myself display so much emotion. It was a very strange feeling. I guess it still seemed unreal, that it couldn't be happening to me even though the surgery was just an hour or so away.

The surgery affected me in more than just the loss of my breast. I was under the anesthetic for four or five hours. I can tell that it has affected my cognitive abilities. I used to be a voracious reader, but I don't sit down and read books the way I used to. I can read, but I just don't. Words don't come to me as quickly. Sometimes the word I'm searching for is right there "on the tip of my tongue," and it just doesn't come to me.

How I looked really bothered me after surgery. I had the mastectomy and a TRAM flap reconstruction all done at the same time. In retrospect, that is a decision that I firmly believe was correct. At the time, however, just out of the hospital and still feeling the trauma of having "cancer," when I looked in the mirror and saw the fresh scars from the mastectomy and the incision from hipbone to hipbone across my lower abdomen, I felt like Frankenstein's monster. Thank the Lord, that feeling quickly faded, and I don't even think about that any more. On the morning of September 12, 2000, as I prepared to leave my home for surgery, a mastectomy, reconstruction, disfigurement, possible chemotherapy, maybe even death, I recalled a small Survival Bible that I had bought a long time ago. I had never even opened it. Sure enough, it had a section on surviving cancer, and there was Nahum 1:7.

"The Lord is good, a refuge in time of trouble, He cares for those who trust in Him."

That obscure verse in a book of the Bible I hardly knew existed became my "refuge in time of trouble."

God certainly cared for us during that traumatic time. We were overwhelmed as Christ ministered to us through His church. We saw His presence in those who visited and in those who prayed for us. In the middle of one of the long nights right after I came home from the hospital, I woke up feeling frightened, cold, and alone. I prayed for the Lord to comfort me. I immediately felt the Holy Spirit fill me with warmth and assurance. I have not been afraid since.

I am now seven years out from breast cancer. My mammograms are good, and my prognosis is good. I can look back now and see how God blessed my husband and me even as we struggled with breast cancer. Second Corinthians 12:9 has helped me put my foolish pride in being independent, in control, and self-reliant in the trash can where it belongs. God is in control, and it is His strength that blesses and keeps us. We praise God for His goodness, for His comfort in times of trouble, and for His care of those who trust in Him and in the wondrous cross of Jesus Christ our Savior.

The following books left their imprint on my heart. I hope you find one or more of them encouraging.

My Book for Kids with Cancer: A Child's Autobiography of Hope by Jason Gaes (Aberdeen, SD: Melius and Peterson Publishers, 1987)

The Race Is Run One Step at a Time: Every Woman's Guide to Taking Charge of Breast Cancer & My Personal Story by Nancy G. Brinker and Catherine McEvilly Harris (Arlington, TX: Summit Publishing Group, revised edition, 1995)

Living with Dying: A Guide for Relatives and Friends by Glen W. Davidson (Minneapolis, MN: Augsburg Fortress Publishers, 1990)

Everyday Strength: A Cancer Patient's Guide to Spiritual Survival by Randy Becton (Grand Rapids, MI: Baker Books, 2006)

When Your Friend Gets Cancer: How You Can Help by Amy Harwell and Kristine Tomasik (Wheaton, IL: Harold Shaw Publishers, 1987)

Damaged But Not Broken: A Personal Testimony of How to Deal with the Impact of Cancer by Larry Burkett and Michael E. Taylor (Chicago, IL: Moody Press, 1996)

Come Away My Beloved by Frances J. Roberts (Uhrichsville, OH: Barbour Publishing, 2002)

The Bible

One more thing about choosing resources. There's a lot of reading material out there, much of which is not beneficial for one reason or another. Keep in mind these tips when choosing resources:

1. Is this information realistically encouraging?
2. Is this information medically sound?
3. Does this resource conflict with God's Word?
4. Is this beneficial to me personally?

Ahh, the Bible! Always a good source. God's Word has supernatural power. Hebrews 4:12 says it is "living and active," and it is. When you take it to heart, you will never be unchanged by it. Read it as God intended — as His words of love and commitment to you. Along with my regular journal, I kept a journal of favorite verses. Here are some Scriptures that saw me through the days of 1990 and still lift me up today.

I am not worthy of all the unfailing love and faithfulness you have shown to me, your servant. GENESIS 32:10; NLT

My presence shall go with you, and I will give you rest. EXODUS 33:14; NASB

Acquaint yourself with Him, and be at peace; thereby good will come to you. . . . For then you will have your delight in the Almighty, and lift up your face to God. JOB 22:21–26; NKJV

In the morning, O LORD, you hear my voice; in the morning I lay my requests before you and wait in expectation. PSALM 5:3; NIV
I will praise the LORD, who counsels me; even at night my heart instructs me. I have set the LORD always before me. Because he is at my right hand, I shall not be shaken. PSALM 16:7–8; NIV

May the words of my mouth and the meditation of my heart be pleasing to you, O LORD, my rock and my redeemer. PSALM 19:14; NLT

I am still confident of this: I will see the goodness of the Lord in the land of the living. Wait for the Lord; be strong and take heart and wait for the Lord. PSALM 27:13–1; NIV

How precious is your unfailing love, O God! All humanity finds shelter in the shadow of your wings. PSALM 36:7; NLT

Mark the blameless [woman], and observe the upright; for the future of that [woman] is peace. PSALM 37:37; NKJV

But the salvation of the righteous is from the Lord; He is [your] strength in time of trouble. And the Lord helps [you] and delivers [you]; He delivers [you] from the wicked and saves [you], because [you] take refuge in Him. PSALM 37:39–40; NASB

The Lord will command His lovingkindness in the daytime; And His song will be with me in the night, a prayer to the God of my life. . . . Why are you in despair, O my soul? And why have you become disturbed within me? Hope in God, for I shall yet praise Him, the help of my countenance, and my God. PSALM 42:8–11; NASB

God is our refuge and strength, a very present help in trouble. Therefore we will not fear, even though the earth be removed, and though the mountains be carried into the midst of the sea. PSALM 46:1–2; NKJV

God is within her, she will not fall; God will help her at break of day. PSALM 46:5; NIV

Be still, and know that I am God! PSALM 46:10; NLT

Cast your cares on the LORD and he will sustain you; he will never let the righteous fall. PSALM 55:22; NIV

When I am afraid, I will put my trust in Thee. PSALM 56:3; NASB

Trust in him at all times, O people; pour out your hearts to him, for God is our refuge. PSALM 62:8; NIV
Teach us to realize the brevity of life, so that we may grow in wisdom.
PSALM 90:12; NLT

Satisfy us in the morning with your unfailing love, that we may sing for joy and be glad all our days. PSALM 90:14; NIV

When doubts filled my mind, your comfort gave me renewed hope and cheer.
PSALM 94:19; NLT

Bless the LORD, O my soul; and all that is within me, bless His holy name! Bless the LORD, O my soul, and forget not all His benefits: Who forgives all your iniquities, who heals all your diseases. PSALM 103:1–3; NKJV

He will have no fear of bad news; his heart is steadfast, trusting in the LORD.
PSALM 112:7; NIV

I will offer to You the sacrifice of thanksgiving, and will call upon the name of the LORD. PSALM 116:17; NKJV

It is good for me that I have been afflicted, that I may learn Your statutes.
PSALM 119:71; NKJV

I rise before dawn and cry for help; I have put my hope in your word.
PSALM 119:147; NIV

He grants sleep to those he loves. PSALM 127:2; NIV

I will bow down toward your holy temple and will praise your name for your love and your faithfulness, for you have exalted above all things your name and your word. When I called, you answered me; you made me bold and stouthearted.
PSALM 138:2–3; NIV

Set a guard, O Lord, over my mouth; Keep watch over the door of my lips.
PSALM 141:3; NKJV

When my spirit grows faint within me, it is you who know my way.
PSALM 142:3; NIV

Teach me to do your will, for you are my God; may your good Spirit lead me on level ground. PSALM 143:10; NIV

Do not put your trust in princes, in mortal men, who cannot save. When their spirit departs, they return to the ground; on that very day their plans come to nothing. Blessed is he whose help is the God of Jacob, whose hope is in the Lord his God. PSALM 146:3–5; NIV

No grave trouble will overtake the righteous. PROVERBS 12:21; NKJV

The light of the righteous shines brightly. PROVERBS 13:9; NIV

A cheerful look brings joy to the heart, and good news gives health to the bones.
PROVERBS 15:30; NIV

Even a fool is thought wise if he keeps silent, and discerning if he holds his tongue.
PROVERBS 17:28; NIV

In quietness and trust is your strength. ISAIAH 30:15; NASB

Fear not, for I have redeemed you; I have summoned you by name; you are mine. When you pass through the waters, I will be with you; and when you pass through the rivers, they will not sweep over you. When you walk through the fire, you will not be burned; the flames will not set you ablaze. For I am the LORD, your God, the Holy One of Israel, your Savior. ISAIAH 43:1–3; NIV
Let him who walks in the dark, who has no light, trust in the name of the LORD and rely on his God. ISAIAH 50:10; NIV

Ah Lord GOD! Behold, Thou hast made the heavens and the earth by Thy great power and by Thine outstretched arm! Nothing is too difficult for Thee.
JEREMIAH 32:17; NASB

This I recall to my mind, therefore I have hope. Through the LORD's mercies we are not consumed, because His compassions fail not. They are new every morning; Great is Your faithfulness. "The LORD is my portion," says my soul, "Therefore I hope in Him!" The LORD is good to those who wait for Him, to the soul who seeks Him. LAMENTATIONS 3:21–25; NKJV

Your Father knows what you need, before you ask Him. MATTHEW 6:8; NASB

May the God of hope fill you with all joy and peace as you trust in him, so that you may overflow with hope by the power of the Holy Spirit. ROMANS 15:13; NIV

My grace is sufficient for you, for My strength is made perfect in weakness. 2 CORINTHIANS 12:9; NKJV

Rejoice in the Lord always. I will say it again: Rejoice! Let your gentleness be evident to all. The Lord is near. Do not be anxious about anything, but in everything, by prayer and petition, with thanksgiving, present your requests to God. And the peace of God, which transcends all understanding, will guard your hearts and your minds in Christ Jesus. PHILIPPIANS 4:4–7; NIV

I can do all things through Him who strengthens me. PHILIPPIANS 4:13; NASB

Always be joyful. Never stop praying. Be thankful in all circumstances, for this is God's will for you who belong to Christ Jesus. 1 THESSALONIANS 5:16–18; NLT

I will never leave you nor forsake you. HEBREWS 13:5; NKJV

Cast all your anxiety on him because he cares for you. 1 PETER 5:7; NIV

Photo Credits